KYLIAN MBAPPÉ

SOCCER SUPERSTAR

BY DEREK MOON

Copyright © 2025 by Press Room Editions. All rights reserved. No part of this book may be used or reproduced in any manner whatsoever, including internet usage, without written permission from the copyright owner, except in the case of brief quotations embodied in critical articles and reviews.

Book design by Jake Nordby
Cover design by Jake Nordby

Photographs ©: Lionel Urman/Abaca Press/Sipa USA/AP Images, cover, 1; Shaun Botterill/Getty Images Sport/Getty Images, 4, 14; Catherine Ivill/Getty Images Sport/Getty Images, 6; Srdjan Stevanovic/Getty Images Sport/Getty Images, 8; Jean Catuffe/Getty Images Sport/Getty Images, 11, 12; Matthias Hangst/Getty Images Sport/Getty Images, 17; Marc Atkins/Getty Images Sport/Getty Images, 18; Clive Rose/Getty Images Sport/Getty Images, 20–21; Laurent Zabulon/Abaca Press/Sipa USA/AP Images, 22, 30; Richard Heathcote/Getty Images Sport/Getty Images, 25; Christian Liewig/Corbis/Getty Images Sport/Getty Images, 27; Red Line Editorial, 29

Press Box Books, an imprint of Press Room Editions, Inc.

ISBN
978-1-63494-952-1 (library bound)
978-1-63494-966-8 (paperback)
978-1-63494-993-4 (epub)
978-1-63494-980-4 (hosted ebook)

Library of Congress Control Number: 2024940742

Distributed by North Star Editions, Inc.
2297 Waters Drive
Mendota Heights, MN 55120
www.northstareditions.com

Printed in the United States of America
012025

About the Author

Derek Moon is an author who lives in Watertown, Massachusetts, with his wife and daughter.

TABLE OF CONTENTS

CHAPTER 1
A Star Is Born 5

CHAPTER 2
Rising to the Top 9

CHAPTER 3
Prince of Paris 15

SPECIAL FEATURE
World Cup Clincher 21

CHAPTER 4
Global Sensation 23

Timeline • 28
At a Glance • 30
Glossary • 31
To Learn More • 32
Index • 32

1 A STAR IS BORN

With each step, Kylian Mbappé moved faster and faster. A misplayed pass had left a loose ball deep in his team's half. The 19-year-old French star darted toward it. Seconds later, he stormed into the opposing penalty area. Sprinting Argentina defenders looked like statues next to Mbappé. The Argentines were desperate to prevent a goal. So, one of the defenders finally dragged Mbappé down.

Mbappé's play drew a penalty kick. A teammate scored to give France an

Before the 2018 World Cup, Kylian Mbappé had played in 15 games for France.

Mbappé does his signature goal celebration after scoring against Argentina in the 2018 World Cup.

early 1–0 lead in the 2018 World Cup match. Argentina then answered with two goals. France got one back to tie it 2–2. A little more than 30 minutes remained for someone to be the hero.

Much of the match's hype had focused on Lionel Messi. The Argentina forward was one of greatest players ever. Yet as the game went on, Mbappé began to command the attention.

In the 64th minute, the ball dropped to Mbappé in the penalty area. In a flash, he cut away from the defenders. His left-footed blast slipped under the goalkeeper. That put France up 3-2. Four minutes later, Mbappé raced up the right wing. A pass led him into the penalty area. The teen met it with a perfectly timed right-footed strike. Just like that, he had doubled France's lead.

Les Bleus (The Blues) held on to win 4-3. Argentina was eliminated. That meant Messi, the sport's most famous star, was headed home. But soccer's next great star was just getting started.

JUST LIKE PELÉ

Pelé won a record three World Cups with Brazil. At age 17, he scored twice in the 1958 final. A few other teenagers scored in World Cups after that. However, none scored twice in one game. Then Kylian Mbappé did it against Argentina. Mbappé later joined Pelé as the second teen to score in the final.

2 RISING TO THE TOP

France won its first World Cup in July 1998. The triumph came on home soil in Paris. Kylian Mbappé was born on December 20, 1998, in the same city. He grew up nearby in Bondy. The suburb was home to many immigrants. That included Kylian's family. His dad was born in Cameroon. His mom's family had come from Algeria.

Kids in Bondy faced many challenges. Soccer became an escape for a lot of them. Kylian began playing at age six.

Kylian Mbappé first played for France's youth team when he was 15.

SUBURBS TO STARDOM

The immigrant-rich Paris suburbs have become a soccer hotbed. Scouts from Clairefontaine regularly search the area for talent. Many players from these suburbs have gone on to become professionals. Midfielders N'Golo Kanté and Paul Pogba are among those who starred for the French national team.

His skills stood out right away. He could easily slip past defenders with his speed. Even older players couldn't stop him. Before long, he had outgrown AS Bondy, his small local club. In 2011, he accepted an invitation to join Clairefontaine. That is France's national soccer academy.

Clairefontaine is known for developing talented young players. Kylian impressed at the academy. Top clubs took notice. Many teams wanted to sign him. In 2013, he picked AS Monaco. The team played in France's best league, Ligue 1. In December 2015, Kylian

Kylian Mbappé recorded 27 goals and 16 assists in his two seasons with AS Monaco.

made his debut for the team. It came days before his 17th birthday.

Kylian Mbappé quickly showed he belonged at that level. In 2016–17, he led Monaco to its best season in years. The teenager played in 29 league games. He

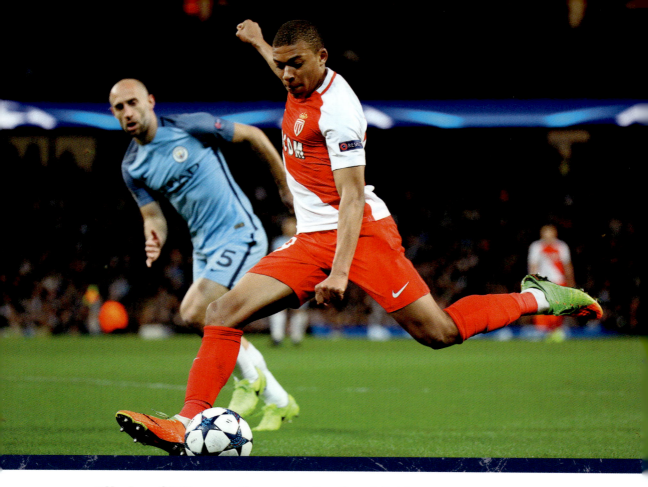

All six of Mbappé's goals in the 2016–17 Champions League came in the knockout stage.

recorded 15 goals and 11 assists. That helped lift Monaco to its first Ligue 1 title in 17 years. Mbappé also caught fire in the Champions League. He scored six goals across nine games. Monaco lost in the semifinals. But it was a magical run. Only once had the team done better in Europe's championship tournament.

By the time he turned 18, Mbappé was one of the brightest young stars in the world. People were comparing him to French legend Thierry Henry. Both players got their start at Monaco. And both seemed to float around the field with ease. Scoring goals came naturally to Mbappé. He put up better stats than Henry had done at that age.

Meanwhile, new owners had taken over Paris Saint-Germain (PSG) in 2011. They sought to turn the team into a European power. Mbappé became central to that vision. In 2017, PSG paid a massive transfer fee to bring Mbappé home. In his first season, he helped the team win the 2018 Ligue 1 title. By the end of that summer, he would be a global superstar.

3 PRINCE OF PARIS

No prize in soccer is bigger than the World Cup. The French team arrived at the 2018 tournament loaded with talent. The forward line was especially skilled. But many fans wondered if the players could come together as one. That had been a problem for France in recent years.

The group stage inspired little confidence. Kylian Mbappé scored in France's second game. That made him the country's youngest goal-scorer in a World Cup. However, France scored just

Mbappé started in six of France's seven games at the 2018 World Cup.

two other goals in the first three games. Les Bleus advanced with two narrow wins and a 0-0 draw.

The team broke out in the round of 16. Mbappé's two goals highlighted a 4-3 win over Argentina. Then France shut out Uruguay and Belgium. That set up a final against Croatia. This time, the French showed their full ability. Mbappé seemed to fly around the field. Danger lurked every time he touched the ball. He scored the fourth goal in a comfortable 4-2 victory. France had won its second World Cup title. The 19-year-old headed back to Paris as one of the biggest stars in the world.

PSG had been a team on the rise. Mbappé kept pushing it higher. In 2018-19, he scored 33 goals in 29 league games. PSG easily defended its Ligue 1 title. Then the team won

Mbappé kisses the World Cup trophy after winning the competition in 2018.

the title again in 2020. PSG also reached its first Champions League final that year. Mbappé scored five goals along the way.

17

Mbappé scored seven goals in the Champions League knockout round before he turned 21.

Still just 20 years old, Mbappé was dominating Ligue 1. However, people began to wonder how long he'd stay. Growing up,

18

posters of Real Madrid players had covered his bedroom wall. The Spanish giants had long been interested in Mbappé, too. Rumors began to swirl in 2021. PSG had just finished second in Ligue 1. Mbappé asked to leave the club that summer.

Instead, PSG brought in superstar Lionel Messi that August. He joined Mbappé and Neymar. They created one of soccer's flashiest forward lines. Together, they led PSG back to the top of Ligue 1. With 28 goals, Mbappé won his fourth scoring title in five seasons. And in May 2022, he agreed to a three-year extension at PSG.

THE RISE OF PSG

Paris is one of Europe's great cities. It's filled with art and culture. Yet for a time, the city had no major men's soccer clubs. PSG began play in 1970. It won Ligue 1 just twice through 2011. Wealthy new owners took over that year. From 2013 to 2024, PSG won 10 league titles.

WORLD CUP CLINCHER

France took a 3–1 lead over Croatia in the 59th minute of the 2018 World Cup final. A few minutes later, France was attacking again. Defender Lucas Hernández controlled the ball on the left wing. Under pressure, he passed to Kylian Mbappé. The teen received the ball just outside the penalty area. No Croatia players were close. Mbappé took two touches on the ball. Then he threaded a long shot between two defenders and past the goalie. It proved too much for Croatia to overcome. France held on to win 4–2.

4 GLOBAL SENSATION

Defending champions often struggle in the World Cup. In 2022, Kylian Mbappé played like he was determined to change that. He scored with ease throughout the tournament. His inspired play led France back to the final. There, Les Bleus faced Argentina. Many fans looked forward to the rematch between Mbappé and Lionel Messi. Both superstars were at the top of their games. Each had scored five goals already. That was tied for the tournament lead.

Mbappé scored multiple goals in three different games during the 2022 World Cup.

Messi struck first in the final. By halftime, the Argentines held a comfortable 2-0 lead. Mbappé still believed, though. In the locker room, he rose to his feet and began rallying his teammates. At 23, he was one of France's youngest starters. But as the game went on, he willed his team forward. France finally got a break in the 80th minute. Mbappé scored on a penalty kick. Then he scored again on a volley 97 seconds later.

The game went into extra time. Messi scored again. But so did Mbappé. The Frenchman's third goal came on another penalty kick. It also gave him a

SIGNATURE CELEBRATION

Kylian Mbappé scores often. And when he does, he usually crosses his arms. Then he tucks his hands into his armpits. Sometimes he does it while sliding. The move was inspired by his younger brother, Ethan. Ethan used to do it after scoring in the *FIFA* video games.

Mbappé strikes the ball to score his second goal of the 2022 World Cup final.

hat trick. Only one other man had done that in a World Cup final. The game went on to a shootout. Both Messi and Mbappé converted their shots. Argentina eventually prevailed. The loss was disappointing for France. However, the performance only confirmed Mbappé's place as one of the world's best.

Talent had never been a question for Mbappé. Pressure didn't seem to bother him either. No matter the situation, he remained in control and ready to score. In March 2023, Mbappé found the net for the 201st time with PSG. No one in club history had scored more. However, all was not well between the player and club. Rumors of Mbappé leaving the team continued. He was still signed with PSG. But he said he would leave after the 2023–24 season. This made club officials angry. They briefly benched the superstar.

In the end, Mbappé did what he always did. With 27 goals, he earned a sixth Ligue 1 scoring title. PSG won its third straight league title as well. After the season, Mbappé signed

Mbappé scored 256 goals in 308 career games with PSG.

with Real Madrid. The kid from Paris had taken his hometown team to new heights. Now he hoped to soar even higher with one of the world's most successful clubs.

TIMELINE

1. Paris, France (December 20, 1998)
Kylian Mbappé is born.

2. Fontvieille, Monaco (December 2, 2015)
At 16, Kylian makes his Ligue 1 debut for AS Monaco.

3. Dortmund, Germany (April 12, 2017)
Mbappé scores twice against Borussia Dortmund in a Champions League quarterfinal game. The following week, he scores again in the home leg to help Monaco advance to the semifinal.

4. Paris, France (August 31, 2017)
Mbappé joins Paris Saint-Germain on loan. The move becomes permanent the following year.

5. Moscow, Russia (July 15, 2018)
Mbappé scores to help France defeat Croatia 4–2. The win gives France its second World Cup title.

6. Lusail, Qatar (December 18, 2022)
In the World Cup final, Mbappé scores twice in regulation and once in extra time. He also converts his penalty in a shootout. However, France falls to Argentina.

7. Paris, France (March 4, 2023)
In a home game against Nantes, Mbappé scores his 201st goal for PSG to become the club's all-time leading scorer.

8. Madrid, Spain (July 16, 2024)
Mbappé is introduced as a Real Madrid player.

MAP

AT A GLANCE

Birth date: December 20, 1998

Birthplace: Paris, France

Position: Forward

Preferred foot: Right

Size: 5-foot-10 (178 cm), 165 pounds (75 kg)

National team: France

Current team: Real Madrid (2024–)

Previous teams: AS Monaco (2015–18), Paris Saint-Germain (2018–24)

Major awards: World Cup Best Young Player (2018), Ligue 1 Player of the Year (2019, 2021–24), World Cup Golden Boot (2022), World Cup Silver Ball (2022)

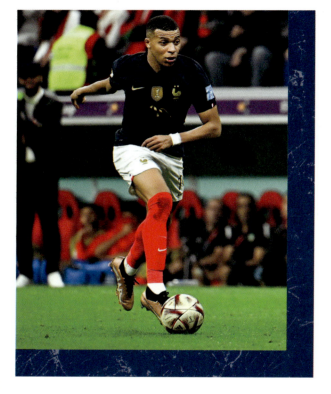

Accurate through the 2023–24 season.

GLOSSARY

academy
A program set up by a soccer team to develop young players.

debut
First appearance.

extra time
Two 15-minute halves that take place if a knockout game is tied after 90 minutes of play.

hat trick
When a player scores three or more goals in a game.

penalty area
The 18-yard box in front of the goal where a player is granted a penalty kick if he or she is fouled.

penalty kick
A kick taken 12 yards away from the goal. The kick is usually awarded after a foul in the penalty area. It is also used to settle a tied match.

scouts
People who look for talented young players.

shootout
A way of deciding a tie game. Players from each team take a series of penalty kicks.

transfer fee
Money that one team pays to another team to gain the rights to a player.

volley
When a player kicks the ball while it's in the air.

TO LEARN MORE

Books

Hanlon, Luke. *The Best Men's Players of World Soccer*. Minneapolis: Abdo Publishing, 2024.

Olson, Ethan. *Great FIFA World Cup Matches*. San Diego: BrightPoint, 2024.

Van Cleave, Ryan G. *Kylian Mbappé: Soccer Icon*. North Mankato, MN: Capstone Press, 2025.

More Information

To learn more about Kylian Mbappé, go to **pressboxbooks.com/AllAccess.**

These links are routinely monitored and updated to provide the most current information available.

INDEX

Argentina, 5–7, 16, 23–25
AS Bondy, 10
AS Monaco, 10–13

Belgium, 16

Champions League, 12–13, 17
Clairefontaine, 10
Croatia, 16, 21

Henry, Thierry, 13
Hernández, Lucas, 21

Kanté, N'Golo, 10

Mbappé, Ethan, 24
Messi, Lionel, 6–7, 19, 23–25

Neymar, 19

Paris Saint-Germain (PSG), 13, 16–17, 19, 26
Pelé, 7
Pogba, Paul, 10

Real Madrid, 19, 27

Uruguay, 16